TEXT FAILS

THE HILARIOUS WORLD OF THE AUTOCORRECTED TEXT MESSAGE
THE BEST COLLECTION OF FUNNIEST TEXT FAIL EVER

Oliver Allen

Copyright © 2020

All right reserved. No portion of this book may be reproduced, stored in a retrieval system, or transmitted in any form or by any means – electronic, mechanical, recording or otherwise – except for brief quotation in printed reviews without the prior written permission of the publisher or the author.

Table of Contents

Introduction 14

*** MOM TEXT FAILS *** 19
ADOPTED 21
AGITATIONS 22
AUTO ERECT 23
BEST TEXT 24
BETTY 25
BIOLOGY 26
BONER 27
CALCULUS 28
CHEWING GUM 29
CHRISTMAS 30
COLD 31
COMING OUT 32
CREDIT CARD 33
CRUEL 34
DAYS OF THE WEEK 35
DECEMBER 36

DIGITAL MOM 37

DOCTOR SEUSS 38

EYES 39

FATHER'S DAY 40

FRIDAY NIGHT 41

GIRAFFE 42

GOOGLE 43

GPS 44

GRAMMAR 45

GRANDMA 46

GROW 47

HOMEMADE 48

HUG 49

HUNGRY 50

INNOCENT 51

JOINT 52

JOKE 53

JUICES 54

KITCHEN 55

LIBRARIAN 56

NEVER MIND 57

NEW CAR 58

OLD PIC 59

OPS	60
PASTRIES	61
PIZZA	62
PRESCRIPTION	63
RUSH	64
SEWING	65
SEX	66
SNIPER	67
SPACE	68
SURPRISE PARTY	69
SURPRISE	70
SWIFFER	71
THANKS	72
THRONE OF KINGS	73
THUGS	74
WALMART	75
WHERE ARE YOU	76
*** DAD TEXT FAILS ***	77
$$$	78
A GOOD DAY	79
ANNIVERSARY	80
APRIL FOOLS	81

AUNT	82
BASEBALL	83
BEES	84
BLACKMAIL	85
BUSINESS	86
CALL ME BABY	87
CEREAL	88
COCA	89
CRASH	90
DONUTS	91
FACEBOOK	92
GLASSES	93
HERPES	94
KAYAK	95
LAPTOP	96
LAUNDRY	97
LAWYER	98
MASSAGE	99
MEAT	100
MISTAKE	101
MOTH	102
NEMO	103
NICKNAME	104

ONIONS	105
OPINION	106
PREGNANT	107
PREGO	108
REALITY	109
S3	110
SCIENCE	111
SHOTGUN AND SHOVEL	112
SMILE	113
SONS	114
STRIP CLUB	115
SUCK	116
SWEAR	117
TALKING	118
TEA	119
THE BUTCHER	120
THE CANNIBAL	121
THE EXCUSE	122
THE HAND	123
THE KEY	124
THE RULER	125
VACUUMING	126
WEED	127

WHATS UP 128

WHY ARE YOU GOING THERE 129

*** WIFE AND HUSBAND TEXT FAILS *** 131

BABY SITTER 133

BEARS 134

BROTHER 135

CHIHUAHUA 136

COMPARISON 137

DINNER 138

DIVORCED 139

HAPPY BIRTHDAY 140

HARRY POTTER 141

MONDAY 142

PRESENT 143

SICKNESS 144

THE DRUNK 145

THE FINGER 146

THE OIL 147

THE POET 148

THE TRUTH 149

*** GRANDPARENTS TEXT FAILS *** 151

FOLLICLES 153

GOOD NEWS 154

GRANNY 155

HELP 156

KILL ME 157

LICK BALLS 158

PRESIDENT 159

TANDEM 160

*** BOYFRIENDS TEXT FAILS *** 161

BROKEN BONES 163

BROTHER 164

BYE BYE 165

CONDOM 166

CONTACTS 167

DO WE REMAIN FRIENDS 168

DREAMS 169

DUMPING 170

EMO 171

END OF STORY 172

HEART ATTACK 173

INVENTORY 174

OMG 175

PAIN OLYMPICS 176

PERMISSION 177

STARS 178

TO SHAVE 179

XBOX 180

ZOMBIES 181

*** GIRLFRIENDS TEXT FAILS *** 183

BALLSACK 185

CLEAN 186

DRAFT 187

EX 188

FILM 189

FIRE 190

GIFT 191

GIRLFIENDS 192

LUBE 193

MERRY CHRISTMAS 194

NOT IN SERVICE 195

PANTIES 196

POEM 197

SEXY 198

TAMPON 199

TWIN 200

WORK 201

*** FRIENDS TEXT FAILS *** 203

ACCIDENT 205

BIRD 206

BLACK AND UPRIGHT 207

BYOP 208

CRAIGSLIST 209

DENTIST 210

DRIVER 211

FORESKIN 212

HAIR 213

JITTERS 214

JUST A WORK 215

LOBSTER 216

MEASURE 217

SISTER 218

TESTICLES 219

THE PARTY 220

THE PIC 221

TITS 222

Introduction

Did you ever have dull moments where no one else has something interesting to say? Since you cannot be online all the time, it makes perfect sense to have a handy book of jokes with you all the time.

And this is where my book, Text Fails, comes in. It is a handy tool to keep you and your friends company when you are looking forward to having a good time!

A failed text is always funny, and now that we have social media, it has become easier to share these failed texts as memes.

But why do they attract so much attention?

A text is real, and it is relatable because we all text. At some point, we all have misspelled words or even sent the text to the wrong person!

As phones get more sophisticated, the fun in text fails is that they are ironic. Despite us having access to auto-correct, these features and software can sometimes be the cause of failed text messages.

Funny text messages come in all forms—from the mundane to the morbid, there is no shortage of funny text messages that can send you rolling in laughter.

What if you can access a lot of these from one source? Wouldn't it be a fun thing to have? Not only would you have an accessible collection of text fails that can brighten your day, but you also have a source of jokes that you can share!

And this is exactly what I did in this book. I thought about a lot of funny texts and collected them, too. In this book, you will be treated to a smorgasbord of failed text messages that would put you in a good mood.

We all want to have a mood booster, and this is what I am offering you. My collection is comprised of:

- Parents sending adult stuff to their kids
- Auto-correct fails
- Biology-related jokes
- Grandma jokes
- Boyfriend jokes
- Mom and Dad
- And a whole lot more!

Use this book as a source of funny anecdotes if you are with your friends. It certainly takes off steam and can help you de-stress at any given time.

Swap jokes with your friends while drinking, in the car, or if your friends are simply looking forward to hearing funny jokes.

Text Fails are timeless jokes. They apply to anybody on any walk of life. While there are jokes here leaning towards an adult audience, all it takes is for you to choose which jokes apply to the right audience.

Text Fails is a book that applies to all occasions. You can use these jokes for your speeches, during a party, or even share it in your social media timeline. These jokes are guaranteed to stir emotions in people who see them, and they can help brighten someone's moods.

Position yourself as a master of jokes. Use this book to get ideas and refine them for your specific situation. Text Fails is the only book you need for hilarious text jokes with about 200 funny entries.

Thank you and happy reading!

*** MOM TEXT FAILS ***

ADOPTED

OMG!!!

NOOO!!!

●●●○○ AT&T　6:06 PM　87%

‹ Messages　**Mom**　Details

I've got to tell you something. Are you sitting down?

> I am actually. What's up mom?

Your brother was adopted!

> What??? What are you talking about?

> Why are you telling me this over a text? Call me

Oh, this damn phone. I wrote accepted and the phone changed it. He got accepted to Yale!

AGITATIONS

OMG!!!

NOOO!!!

Mom

Do we have any stain remover or anything

What do you mean? What happened.

I shook my cock too hard and it exploded all over my clothes and floor.

I'm at work Jake. This isn't funny. Call your dad.

Holy crap. I mean Coke. It exploded when I opened it. Do we have Shout or a Tide stick or something?

In the laundry room

AUTO ERECT

OMG!!!

NOOO!!!

●●●○○ Sprint LTE 8:32 AM 75%

< Messages **Mom** Details

dad and I fondled ourselves for the first time last night.

We didn't get good results. nothing came up.

> LMAO, mom, I don't know what you tried to write but that hilarious!!!

!!! damn auto erect !!!

AutoCorrect!!! We googled ourselves! No results!!!

23

BEST TEXT

OMG!!!

NOOO!!!

●●○○○ Sprint LTE   11:27 AM   22%

‹ Messages   **Jimmy**   Details

Jill, I hate your small bush and tiny penis. I'm leaving you for Jack

Mom? its Jimmy

Oops, you never heard a thing. I'll pay you $100

Make it 200 and a new car

Fine you can have 200 and a new car.it don't post this on Facebook I'll give u a new weight set and your own apartment

best text I've ever responded to

iMessage   Send

BETTY

OMG!!!

NOOO!!!

> Messages **Mom** Details
>
> I think I keep getting messages or missed calls or something.
>
> From who?
>
> Some woman named...Betty Low
>
> Uhm, BATTERY LOW?!?!
>
> YEAH, THAT'S IT!!

BIOLOGY

BONER

OMG!!!

NOOO!!!

Mom: Just got off the phone with your brother

Mom: He said you just gave him a boner

Me: Ew, mom WTF? That's sick. Why would u say that

Mom: boner Amanda

Mom: l o a n

Me: Wow mom. You need to learn to text. Yes I gave him $600.

Mom: Boner

27

CALCULUS

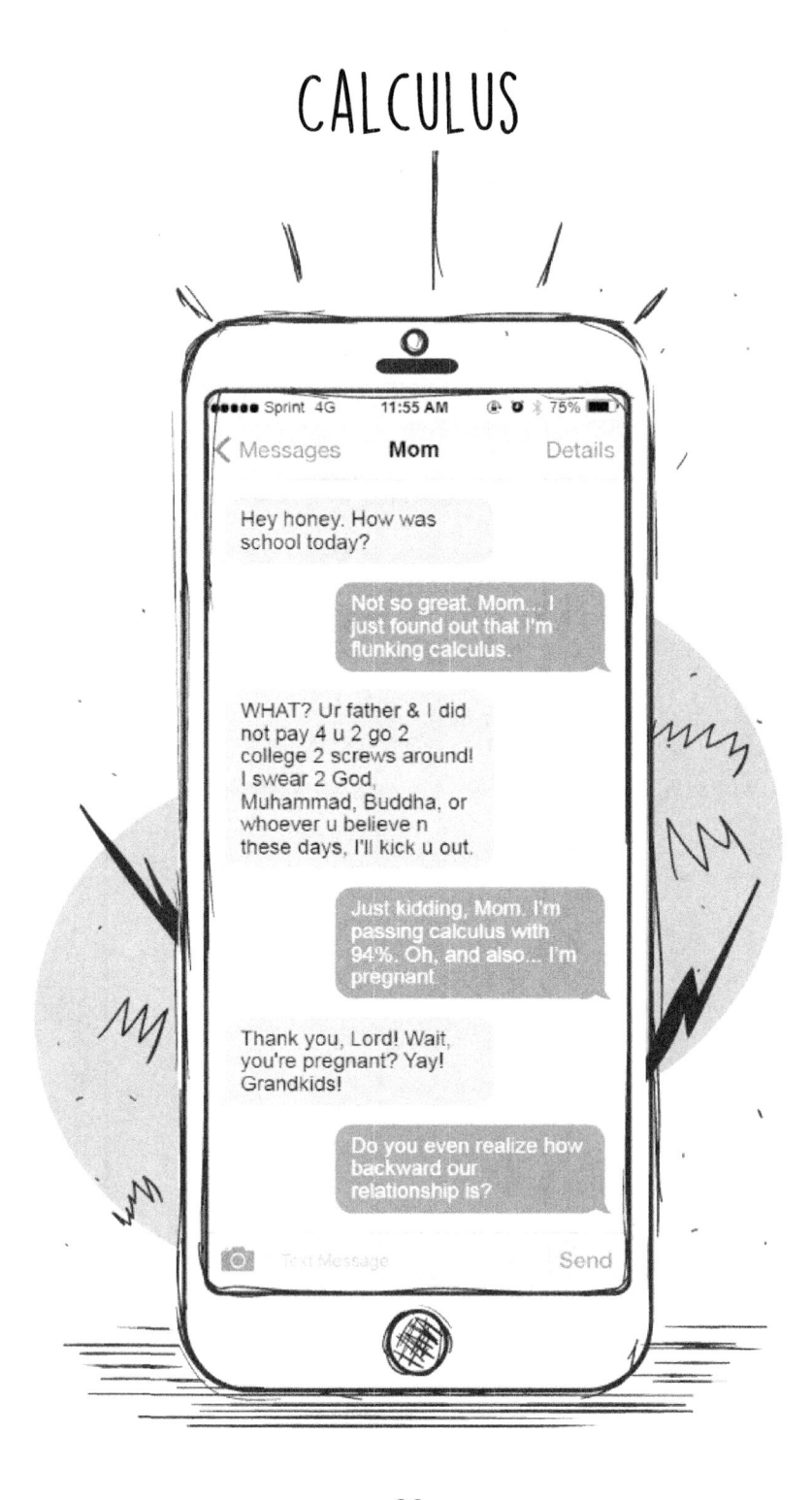

Mom

Hey honey. How was school today?

> Not so great. Mom... I just found out that I'm flunking calculus.

WHAT? Ur father & I did not pay 4 u 2 go 2 college 2 screws around! I swear 2 God, Muhammad, Buddha, or whoever u believe n these days, I'll kick u out.

> Just kidding, Mom. I'm passing calculus with 94%. Oh, and also... I'm pregnant

Thank you, Lord! Wait, you're pregnant? Yay! Grandkids!

> Do you even realize how backward our relationship is?

28

CHEWING GUM

OMG!!!

NOOO!!!

●●○○○ Sprint 3G 5:53 AM 38°F

< Messages **Bella** Details

Worst day ever

Bring some scissors over. Robby got his cum in my hair.

> It's ok. I have had so much cum in my hair. U don't have to cut it. Just wash it.

I meant GUM mom. GUM.

Now I'm gonna throw up!

> I will be over in 2 mins

29

CHRISTMAS

OMG!!!

NOOO!!!

•••• Sprint LTE   4:17 PM   33%

< Messages   **Mom**   Details

You are definitely coming here for Christmas right? I am cooking ham.

Yes - and I'm bringing drugs.

Oh like hell you are.

Don't you even THINK about bringing drugs into this house Melissa.

Wow, chill mom. I meant I'm bringing DOUG.

Well, why didn't you say that

COLD

OMG!!!

NOOO!!!

> My throat hurts

> Sorry. You are pro ably getting a dildo

> A cold!

COMING OUT

OMG!!!

NOOO!!!

●●●○○ Verizon 📶 11:41 AM ○ 45% ▮

‹ Messages **Mom** Details

Hey, mom, I've decided I'm coming out

Oh Michael, Dad and I always knew you were gay. But I am a tad shocked you texted me! I love you no matter what!

MOM. IM NOT GAY. I sent my text before I could finish. I'm coming out to see you and Dad in May!

LOL. We love you no matter what type of coming out you do!

CREDIT CARD

OMG!!!

NOOO!!!

●●○○○ Verizon 4G   11:06 AM   85%

< Messages   **Mom**   Details

Hey, Em do u have my masturbator? Can't find it. Thought I gave it to your daddy, but he says he only has his. Did I let u use it for something?

Omg!! Hahaha!! Mom I N don't want to know about ur masturbator. Read what u sent me.

I meant MasterCard. Do you have my MasterCard. That's embarrassing. L-O-L

Text Message   Send

CRUEL

OMG!!!

NOOO!!!

●●○○○ AT&T LTE 7:22 PM 63%

‹ Messages **Mom** Details

Don't forget to unload the dishwasher

Did you finish your homework?

We have to go to your grandmother's house for Thanksgiving

Dad and I talked, we are going to buy you a car next month.

> U are??? Omg thank u

No. We're not. I just wanted to make sure you were getting my texts.

> That was cruel

DAYS OF THE WEEK

OMG!!!

NOOO!!!

●●○○○ AT&T 4G   5:51 PM

‹ Messages   **Mommie**   Details

When are you coming home?

Hello?? WTF??

> Mom! Do you know what that means?

Yeah, are you coming home Wednesday, Thursday, or Friday?

> OMG -_-

DECEMBER

OMG!!!

NOOO!!!

●●●○○ AT&T LTE　11:15 AM　75%

‹ Messages　**Mommie**　Details

Bro, I just got laid! It was epic!

Look who your texting

Shit...

Get home now

April fools!

It's December get your ass home now!

...

December fools!

HOME NOW!

🗎　Text Message　Send

DIGITAL MOM

OMG!!!

NOOO!!!

Finally, you've entered the digital age and got a smartphone!

How is it?

Mum?

Helloooooo??

Why aren't you answering??

Howdoyoudoaspace

DOCTOR SEUSS

did you oops in the sink

I mean did you poop on the shrink

on the shower

why won't my phone write what I tell it to

did you poop in the shrink

shower

> Um no, I didn't poop in the shower, sink, or on my shrink! Lol

> You sound like doctor Seuss. Calling you

EYES

OMG!!!

NOOO!!!

○○○○ Sprint 3G   10:40 AM   90%

< Messages   **Mommie**   Details

Hey hun, what does this mean??? (.)(.)

o.O in what context

I'm in love with your (.)(.)

Eheheh; Eyes mom. Dad loves your eyes.

Awe that's cute. Thank you =D

Be sure to tell him you enjoy his 8===D Smile

FATHER'S DAY

OMG!!!

NOOO!!!

Mom

Father's Day is coming and I just overheard your dad say he wants a new dick

a new dick

He said he wants a new dick

shit dick

> A new shit dick. Got it. Thanks, mom!

I am calling you.

Why didn't you answer?

FRIDAY NIGHT

OMG!!!

NOOO!!!

Mommie

What are you doing tonight

> Um going to a movie w Joey. What about you?

Dad and I are headed to bed to cuddle up and enjoy some Friday Night lube.

> Ewwwwwwwwwww mom I'm gonna barf.

lol. Friday Night Lights. But that was a funny autocorrect.

> Yeah I'm not laughing

GIRAFFE

OMG!!!

NOOO!!!

Mom

I'm using that shake weight dad gave me. I feel like I am jerking off a giraffe.

Ewwwie mom. Gross

GOOGLE

OMG!!!

NOOO!!!

•••• Sprint LTE   10:29 AM   100%
‹ Messages   **Mom Cell**   Details

please stop changing the google logo so much

I like the original one

> Mom, I don't change the logo. Google changes it.

on my computer

You don't run the google?

> If I did I wouldn't be driving a 2004 ford.

GPS

OMG!!!

NOOO!!!

oooo Verizon 3G   1:40 PM   8%

< Messages   **Mom**   Details

Great news!!!! I finally found my GSPOT.

Um... Wow. Thank you so much for sharing. Congratulations?

I found it in the back seat of my car.

Ok, mom now this is just getting too weird. I know we are close but come on.

Huh?

Oh God! My GPS! Hahaha!!!

GRAMMAR

OMG!!!

NOOO!!!

Mom

Got 2 grams for $40

Nvm wrong person

> 2 grams of what??

> DANIEL ANSWER ME

Grammar books

> Oh I thought you were talking about the weed lol

> Did you have enough money or do you need me to put some more in your account?

A little more wouldn't hurt

GRANDMA

OMG!!!

NOOO!!!

Mom

Your grandma just died. Lol!

> Mom, how is that funny?

What are you talking about? It's not! This is serious.

> Mom, lol means laugh out load.

OH MY GOSH, I thought it meant lots of love! I sent that to everyone!

GROW

OMG!!!

NOOO!!!

●●●●○ Verizon 4G　3:32 PM　　22%

‹ Messages　**Mom**　Details

I fucking hate you, seriously. I'm leaving.

> It's about time you grow up. Your father and I thought you'd never leave. You need to grow a pair of balls and get a girlfriend, too.

Sorry, mom that was supposed to go to Mike.

Wait wtf mom?

Fuck you too!

> I'm cooking your favorite for dinner
>
> tonight bacon burgers. love

Send

47

HOMEMADE

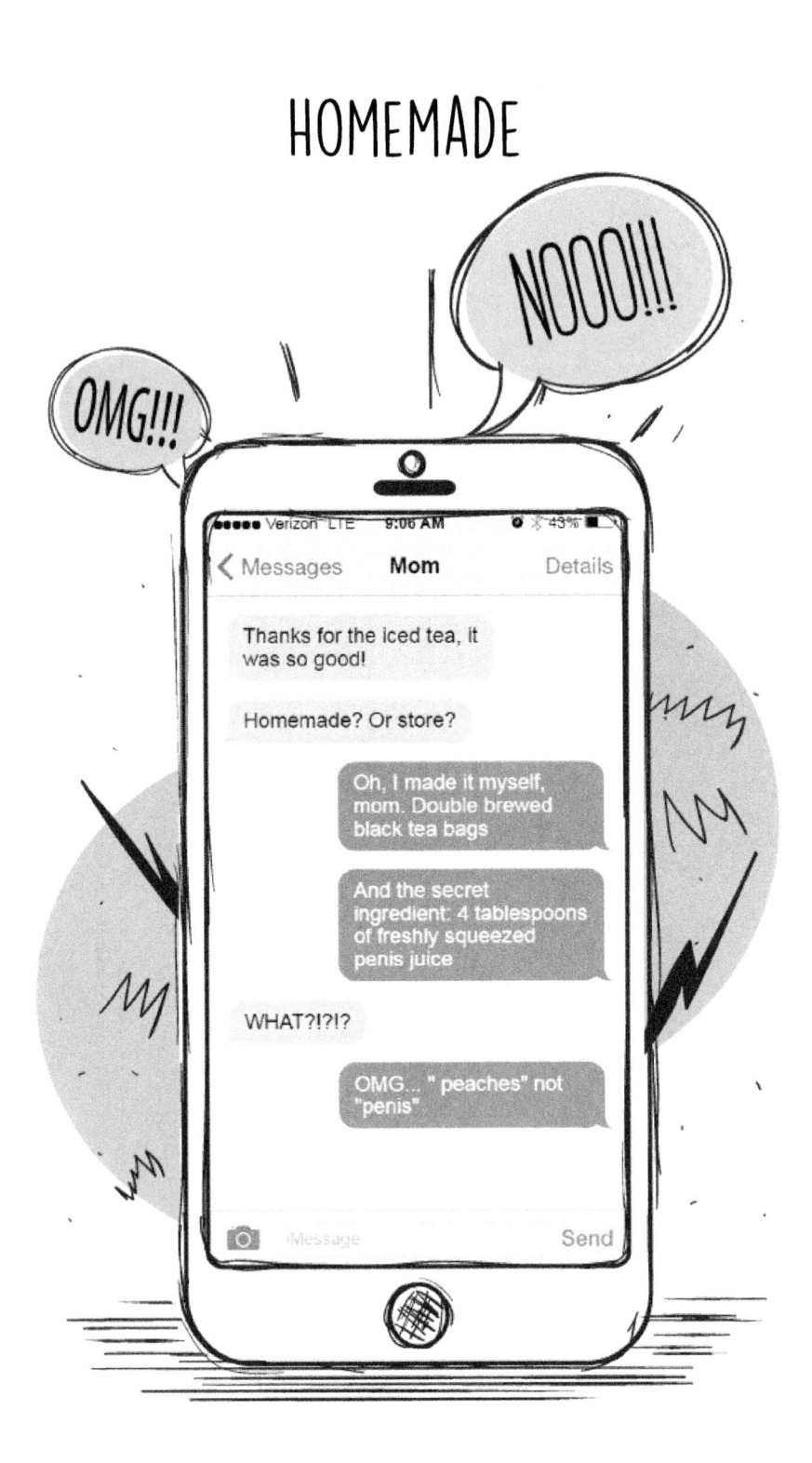

OMG!!!

NOOO!!!

Mom

Thanks for the iced tea, it was so good!

Homemade? Or store?

Oh, I made it myself, mom. Double brewed black tea bags

And the secret ingredient: 4 tablespoons of freshly squeezed penis juice

WHAT?!?!?

OMG... "peaches" not "penis"

HUG

OMG!!!

NOOO!!!

> Not yet
>
> :)(( ))
>
> Mom!!! Do not send that!
>
> A hug?
>
> No look it up. It's a female body part
>
> Wh... Aaaaa!
>
> Yeah

HUNGRY

Mom: are you hungry?

Me: Starving

Mom: I thought you might be. There's a huge surprise waiting for you in the kitchen. It's your favorite. Love Mom.

Me: I hope it's your shaved pussy

Me: Omg

Me: Please don't read that last text it was the worst autocorrect of my life

Me: I meant porkkkkk shaved pork. I'm so sorry Ma

Me: Mom?

INNOCENT

OMG!!!

NOOO!!!

●●●○○ AT&T LTE 6:53 PM @ ○ ☀ 90% ■

‹ Messages **Momma** Details

Come home as soon as you can babe, I'm feeling slutty! ;)

Mom... wtf!!

Oh! Sorry, Hunny. That was meant for your father... Don't pretend like you are all innocent. I've seen the texts u send ur bf, hoe.

Fair enough, bye.

JOINT

OMG!!!

NOOO!!!

oooo Sprint LTE 11:46 AM 22%

< Messages **Mom** Details

Jerry, I just found a joint in your pillow case. You're in big trouble

No, you didn't. Your lying

How do you know?

Cos I keep my joints in the sock drawer

Ah Shit

JOKE

Mom! I think there's a threat to the' house! COME HOME!

> Go and hide in your closet!! NOW! I will be home in 15 minutes!

I can hear steps mom! IM SCARED!

> Just be quiet honey!

Okay, I think he is gone now...phew! But I can't get out of the closet! OMG, HE LOCKED ME IN!!

> No, he didn't, I did. And I came early from the meeting. Omg, you are so easy to scare! PS. I hope that you still talking to me! Love you.-Mom :-)

JUICES

OMG!!!

NOOO!!!

●●●○○ T-Mobile LTE 10:53 PM @ ⊙ ✶ 38% ■

< Messages   **Maria**   Details

Not much! Just drinking this pube juice my mom bought for me today. Yummy right? (:

> Not my first choice in juices.. (:

Granted. It does taste a little funky but other then thAt I could drink this all day! (:

Dude. I meant prune. I swear. (:

> AHAHA. sure... That's what they all say (,

54

KITCHEN

OMG!!!

NOOO!!!

Mom: Why are there cups and dishes in your room? They belong in the kitchen.

Me: Ha, just like a woman

Mom: A woman is more likely to be in the kitchen than in your bedroom

55

LIBRARIAN

OMG!!!

NOOO!!!

●●●○○ Verizon LTE   7:28 PM   42%

‹ Messages   **Mom**   Details

Karen has Lyme disease.

> Who is Karen?

You know Karen.

> Mom, I have no idea who Karen is.

Uh, the librarian when you were in kindergarten.

NEVER MIND

OMG!!!

NOOO!!!

●●○○○ Verizon 3G   8:41 AM   ⚡ 100%

< Messages   **Mom**   Details

Andy, I can't find my phone. Can you call it so I can try to track it down?

> I don't even have time to be quippy, mom. It's in your hand.

What? No, it's not. I've got a bag of groceries in my hand. Are you saying it's in the grocery bag!? How do you know these things!?

> WHAT ARE YOU TEXTING ME WITH!?

Never mind! I found it! Thanks!

NEW CAR

OMG!!!

NOOO!!!

Sprint 3G 10:27 AM 31%
< Messages **Mom** Details

Dad just told me you bought a car! Can you afford that?

YOLO

Do you even know what that means?

No :) But did I use it correctly?

Sadly, yes...

58

OLD PIC

OMG!!!

NOOO!!!

●●●○○ Sprint LTE 7:32 PM 34%

< Messages **Mom B** Details

I just found a pic of you holding your blueballs!

You were so adorable!

I don't recall ever taking that picture mom!!!

Please reread that msg!

I wrote boombox! What is a blueball?

Ask dad

59

OPS

OMG!!!

NOOO!!!

●●●○○ Sprint LTE   7:32 PM   34%

< Messages   **Mom B**   Details

I just found a pic of you holding your blueballs!

You were so adorable!

I don't recall ever taking that picture mom!!!

Please reread that msg!

I wrote boombox! What is a blueball?

Ask dad

iMessage   Send

PASTRIES

OMG!!!

NOOO!!!

•••• Sprint 10:40 AM 11%

‹ Messages **Mom** Details

YOU home ma?

> Yes. I'll be here till 5. Are you stopping by?

Yea. I want you to taste these pussies from new york

> I haven't done that since college. KIDDING!

OMG, mom, that's sick. And my phone is officially perverted

> "pastries" mom, pastries.

PIZZA

OMG!!!

NOOO!!!

Messages — **Mom** — Details

Hey, mom dinner will be ready at 7. Any special requests?

Yes! Please put the sausage on my pussy!

I mean I'd like sausage. On my pussy.

The phone won't let me write pussy!

P.I.Z.Z.A.

I'm so sorry I asked LOL

PRESCRIPTION

Mom

How is Dad? Did you go to the appointment with dr.?

> Okay. He has heartburn. The doctor prescribed prostitutes.

> 2x per day.

Wow. In that case, I have heartburn too. Lol

Best prescription ever!

> Oh gosh. Not funny. Prilosec. That is my worst auto correct ever!

RUSH

OMG!!!

NOOO!!!

Mom

I can't pick you up today. I have thrush.

Ew Mom!

Lol I mean I have to rush

How do you know what thrush is?

SEWING

SEX

OMG!!!

NOOO!!!

oooo Sprint LTE 5:00 PM 32%
< Messages **Mom** Details

baby, u r 14 now, I think its time we talk about sex

k, mom, tell me what u wanna know...

...

SNIPER

OMG!!!

NOOO!!!

Hi mom, just to let you know, I've decided to make some extra money by becoming a sniper

> Oh honey, please don't do that. It's so dangerous. You don't need to be a sniper

You'll be relieved to know that was a spelling mistake and that I'm actually becoming a stripper

SPACE

OMG!!!

NOOO!!!

oooo Sprint 2:17 PM 7%

< Messages **Mom** Details

Hi, Bridget, I space space space space how space are space you space doing period capital eye love this new phone exclamation point

I see you're using voice text. You don't have to say space mom it does it for you

I cucumber letter pea Ritalin

What? Mom stop just type

iMessage Send

68

SURPRISE PARTY

OMG!!!

NOOO!!!

●●●○○ Verizon 3G   8:07 PM   35%

‹ Messages   **Mom**   Details

How was dads surprise party??

> It was great we scared the cum out of him!!

Jacob that is not funny.

> Omg! I'm so sorry! I meant cum!

> NOOO! I mean crap, we scared the *CRAP out of dad

Ok because the other ones my job :)

SURPRISE

OMG!!!

NOOO!!!

> Matt: Keep a secret be here by 8 PM tomorrow, Joey is going to ask Maya to marry him! I am so terribly excited! Don't be late!

> Holy shit mom. You texted that to me. Joey is going to ask me to marry him tomorrow??? I think you just ruined the greatest surprise of my life.

SWIFFER

OMG!!!

NOOO!!!

•••○○ Sprint 3G   11:17 AM   12%

‹ Messages   **Mom**   Details

I am divorcing your father! LOL

> Oh God what now mom

He gave me a stiffy for our anniversary last night. Unreal.

> A stiffy!!! Ew, mom, I don't need to hear about that.

No, a Swiffer. 30 yrs of marriage for a Swiffer.

What is a stiffy

> Don't even ask. But it's better than a swiffer LOL

THANKS

OMG!!!

NOOO!!!

●●●●○ Sprint 4G   9:46 AM   @ ✻ 42% ■

< Messages   **Mom**   Details

How do I delete the voicemail from the home phone?

Press 7

GRASSY ASS!

What?

GRASSY ASS!

I don't get it.

Spanish for "thanks" right?

Oh you mean gracias! LOL

THRONE OF KINGS

OMG!!!

NOOO!!!

●●●○○ AT&T LTE 7:08 PM 21%

‹ Messages **Mom** Details

Throne of Kings is on again tonight at 9 if you want to watch it

Thank you, honey, but I can't

I'll be in bed. I have to be up at 4 am to do a porno at work tomorrow.

Wow mom, Is money that rough?:)

Not porno! Promo! I don't do pornos at work!

Well, that's a relief!

THUGS

OMG!!!

NOOO!!!

> bought you a couple thugs today for Valentines Day. I will ship them out to you Monday.

> Wow, isn't that a bit overkill to keep the boys away from your little girl?

> OMGM! I meant things. Lol

> Rofl

> I am laughing so hard I have to cross my legs

> Lol don't pee yourself Mommy

WALMART

OMG!!!

NOOO!!!

●●●○○ Verizon 3G　11:29 AM　　15%

< Messages　　**Mom**　　Details

Mom Where are you????

Leaving Walmart. Halfway home. Why sweetie?

You brought me to Walmart with you -_-

OH DARN! Be there in a bit

WHERE ARE YOU

OMG!!!

NOOO!!!

•••○○ Sprint LTE 3:04 PM 75%

< Messages **Mom** Details

Where are you?

> Im at my girlfriend's house

What!?!?!?

> Just kidding I'm in the ghetto selling drugs

Ohhhh ok. You had me worried there. .. So how much have you made?

✳✳✳ DAD TEXT FAILS ✳✳✳

DAD

$$$

NOOO!!!
OMG!!!
Verizon LTE 11:26 AM 24%
Messages
Dad
Details
$chool Is really great. I am making lot$ of friends and $tudying very hard. With all my $tuff, I $imply can't think of anything I need. <3
I kNOw that astroNOmy, ecoNOmics, and oceaNOgraphy are eNOugh to keep even an hoNOr student busy. Do NOt forget that the pursuit of kNOwledge is a NOble task. <3
Fuck.
Get a job.
iMessage
Send

A GOOD DAY

OMG!!!

NOOO!!!

Dad

Hey honey, how's your day?

> Good. I'm having the best weed of my life.

Oh me too...where did you get your's from

> NO NO NO I meant WEEK!!!! Wait what dad?

Let's not tell mom about this conversation...

ANNIVERSARY

OMG!!!

NOOO!!!

Sprint LTE 11:48 AM 100%

Messages **Dad** Details

I can't wait for tomorrow. Anniversary sex is so fucking amazing with you, baby. Mmmm.;)

Dad, this is your son.

I mean, did your mother pick you guys up yet?

No, but she's obviously gonna pick you up tomorrow.

APRIL FOOLS

Dad...I'm pregnant!

April Fools! Sorry sweetie, but I'm not falling for it! Both of your sisters already tried to pull that one on me...

Oh...um...yeah. April Fools... ??

Josh, I tried to tell my father and he thought I was kidding! Maybe you were right..maybe we should run away together.

WHAT?! THIS IS STILL YOU'RE FATHER! YOU ARE NEVER LEAVING THIS HOUSE AGAIN. I'M ASHAMED TO CALL YOU MY DAUGHTER.

April Fools ;)

AUNT

OMG!!!

NOOO!!!

Dad

Your cunt is really annoying to me.

WHAT???!!!???

Your cunt. It is loud and is annoying me.

OMG. Dad are you drunk?

Oops, I meant, your aunt. She is here with your mother. She is screeching while watching American Idol.

Wow, dad. Fail.

BASEBALL

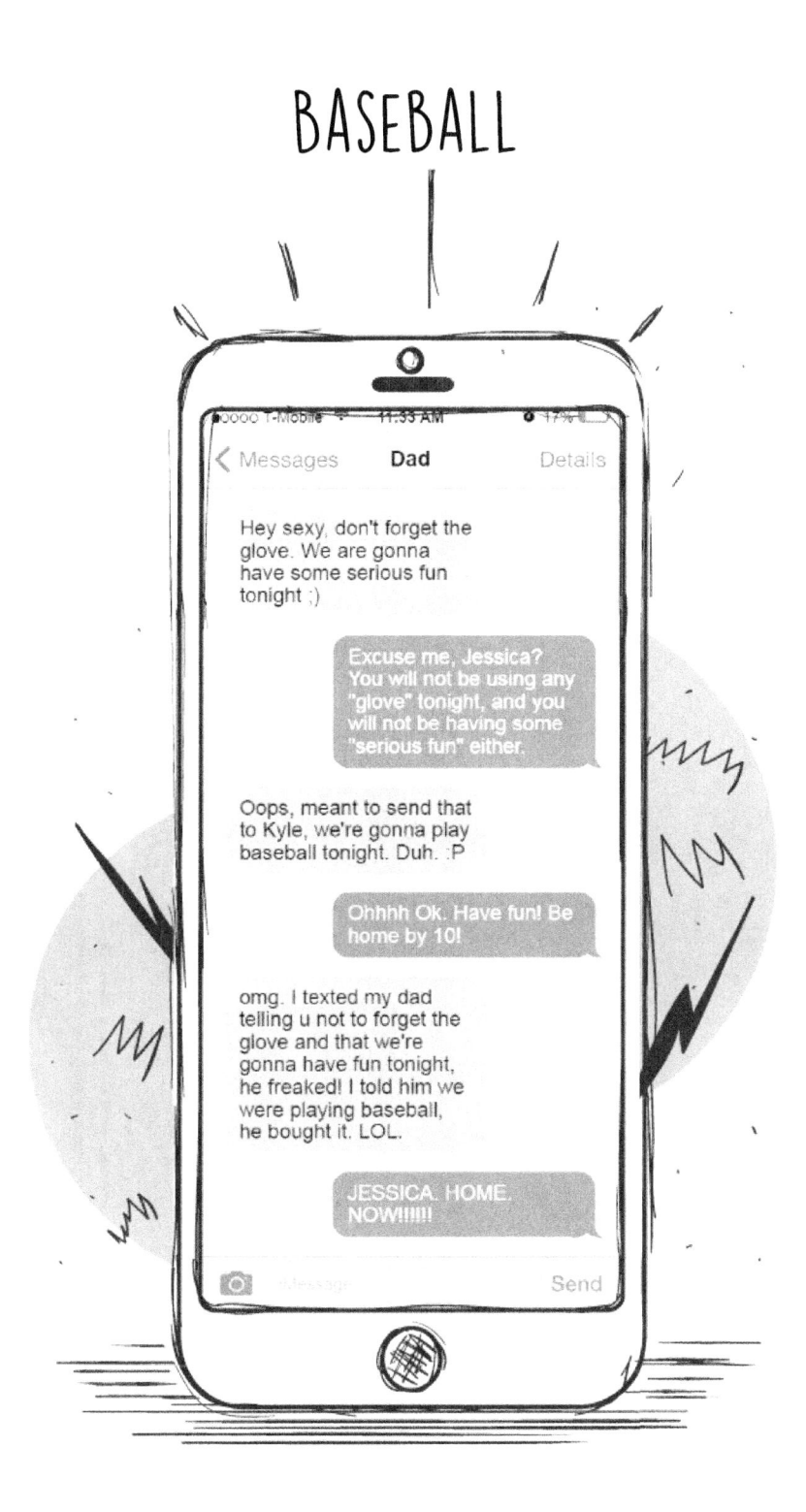

Dad

Hey sexy, don't forget the glove. We are gonna have some serious fun tonight ;)

> Excuse me, Jessica? You will not be using any "glove" tonight, and you will not be having some "serious fun" either.

Oops, meant to send that to Kyle, we're gonna play baseball tonight. Duh. :P

> Ohhhh Ok. Have fun! Be home by 10!

omg. I texted my dad telling u not to forget the glove and that we're gonna have fun tonight, he freaked! I told him we were playing baseball, he bought it. LOL.

> JESSICA. HOME. NOW!!!!!!

BEES

OMG!!!

NOOO!!!

Dad

I heard mom got stung by a few bees this morning. Is she ok??? Hospital???

She is okay now. No hospital.

She had to take the deep penis.

Uh... What?

I had to inject her with an epic penis.

Oh for Christ's sake.

EpiPen

BLACKMAIL

Dad

Hey, Mandy are you ready for tonight? I got the condoms!

> Uhh, dad, this is Mindy, wtf I expect a car, $200, and a new laptop with a camera for me on Monday and I won't tell mom.

How dare you try and blackmail me that was a test and you are grounded for demanding all that stuff!

Hey sorry Mandy I texted my daughter by mistake and told her it was a test and she believed me she is such an idiot. So what time tonight?

> Make that $300 and add an iPad 2, love you, daddy, <3

Shit!

BUSINESS

OMG!!!

NOOO!!!

●●●○○ Sprint LTE 5:42 PM 45%
< Messages **DAD** Details

$20 a gram. The wife's out town for the weekend. Stop by today and tomorrow only.

DAD! YOU,VE GOT TO FUCKING BE KIDDING ME!!!

Shit. I'll give you 25% of what I make if you don't tell mom.

50% or I'll hit the fwd button.

Deal

Pleasure doing business with you

CALL ME BABY

OMG!!!

NOOO!!!

●●○○○ Sprint LTE   6:33 PM   ✱ 12% ⬜

‹ Messages   **Dad**   **Details**

Hey, Jake, Dad's out for the night, so if you want to come over feel free. Just don't forget the lube. ;)

> Alright, baby, I'll see you then.

Did I mention that I love it when you call me baby?

> Did I mention that I loved being called "Daddy"? Check the name, son.

Shit...

> That's alright. Have fun. P.S. I knew you were gay

CEREAL

OMG!!!

NOOO!!!

Dad

Hey dad, forget something a the store?

> Let's see, peanut butter, bread, pancakes. Nope, everything here.

Well, you know there's also cereal and ME!!

> Oh, thanks. I almost forgot cereal.

:-|

COCA

OMG!!!

NOOO!!!

oooo Sprint 3G 5:16 AM @ o ⚡ 85%

< Messages **Dad** Details

hey, dad, can I have some money for coke?

yea sure is $70 enough?

dad, it costs $ 1.50

WOW, prices went down since I was a kid! well, have fun snorting your coke I'm on my way to give you the money now.

WAIT WHAAT?!?!? I'm talking about coca-cola! AND YOUR FINE WITH YOUR SON DOING COCAINE? WTF DAD?!!?!

ill give you $100 to shut up and not tell mom!

CRASH

OMG!!!

NOOO!!!

Messages **Dad** Details

I love you, dad :)

What did you do this time?

Don't get mad but I crashed the car

WTF CHARLOTTE?!?

Mistakes happen!

Yeah just like YOU!

DONUTS

OMG!!!

NOOO!!!

Dad

DAD!

Daddyyyyyy

Omg dad mom just died

Dad... I'm pregnant

We got donuts

> i'll be home in 10 mins. if the donuts aren't there I will be pissed.

FACEBOOK

OMG!!!

NOOO!!!

Messages — **Dad** — Details

Hi. I am fairly new to Facebook. Mind accepting my friend request?

you made a Facebook? WTF!!

What does "WTF" mean?

Oh it means welcome facebook

GLASSES

OMG!!!

NOOO!!!

●●●○○ Sprint LTE 11:33 AM 60% ■
< Messages **Dad** Details

Hey, have you seen where my glasses are?

check your face, Dad

Woah, you must be physic!

No, I just have experience. From you and Grandpa.

Oh alright, by the way, have you seen my phone?

...Dad, PLEASE go back to school for me.

HERPES

OMG!!!

NOOO!!!

Dad

WTF???? Do you have herpes?!? Why the hell didn't you tell me before it was too late to get condoms?

> O.0

Don't gimmie that bullshit!!! what will happen if my wife finds out?

> Ummmmmm... hi dad

50" flatscreen, xbox 360, or $1000

> All and a door lock w/ a subscription to Brazzers

KAYAK

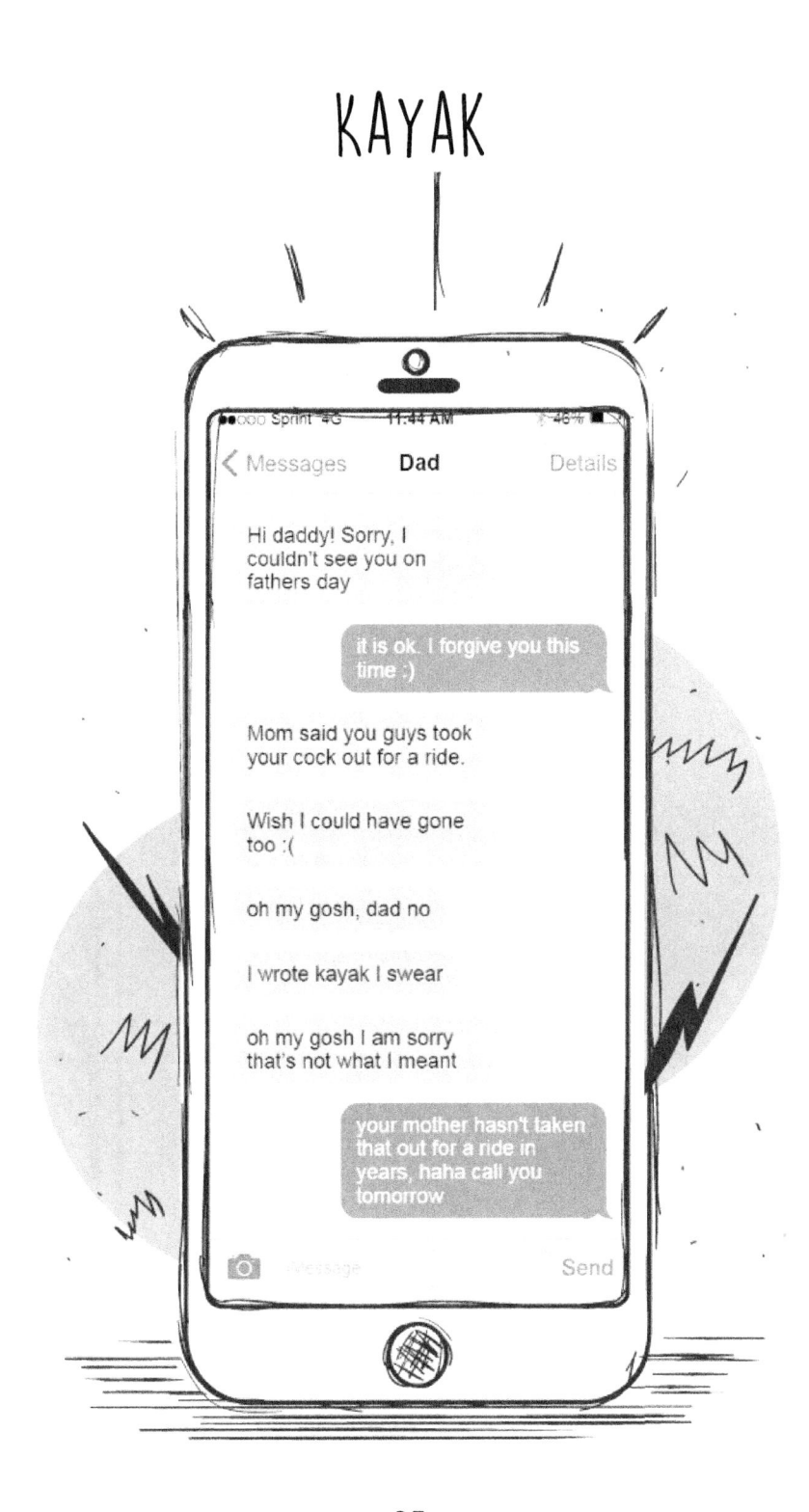

Dad

Hi daddy! Sorry, I couldn't see you on fathers day

> it is ok. I forgive you this time :)

Mom said you guys took your cock out for a ride.

Wish I could have gone too :(

oh my gosh, dad no

I wrote kayak I swear

oh my gosh I am sorry that's not what I meant

> your mother hasn't taken that out for a ride in years, haha call you tomorrow

LAPTOP

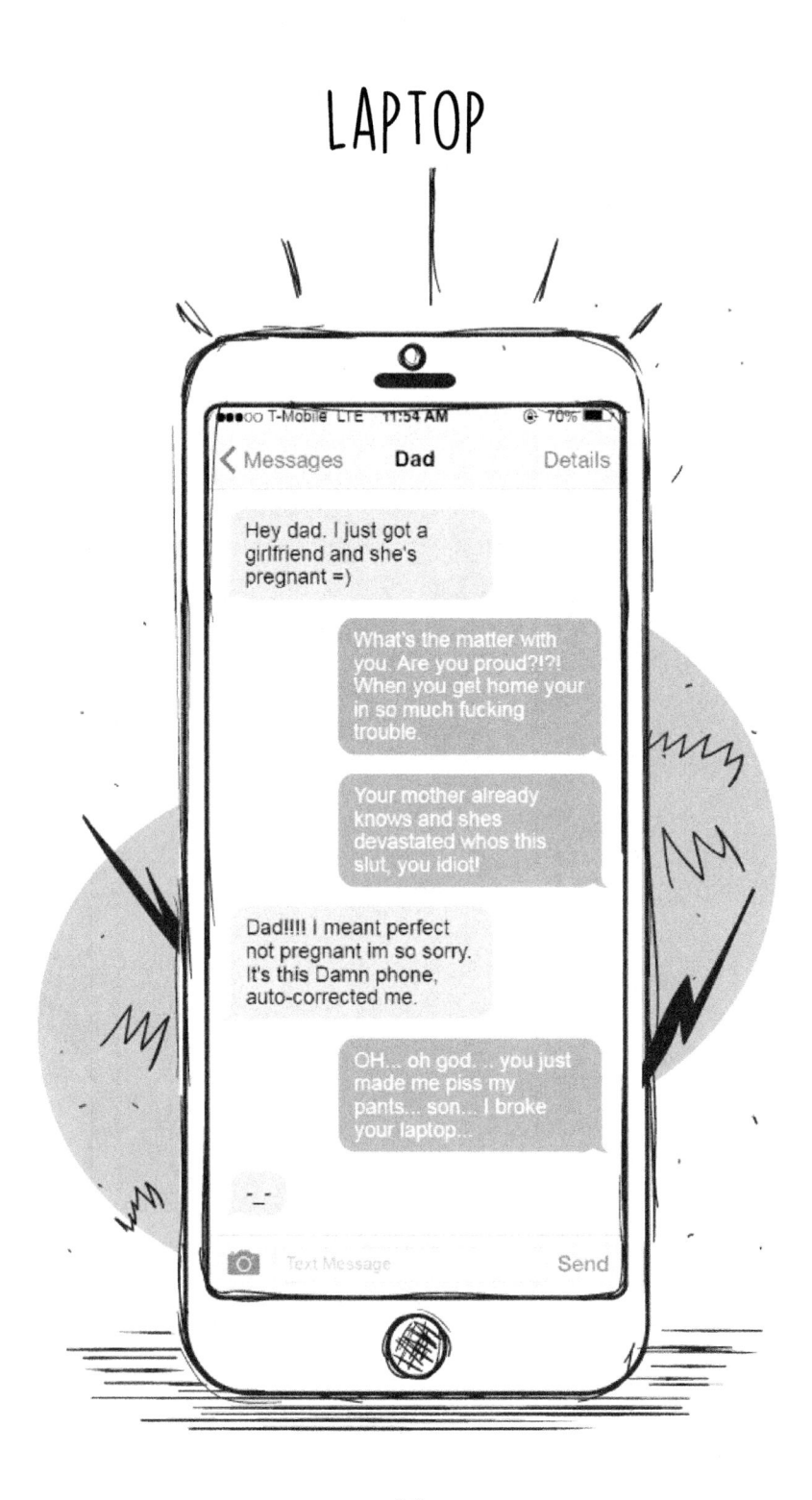

Dad

Hey dad. I just got a girlfriend and she's pregnant =)

What's the matter with you. Are you proud?!?! When you get home your in so much fucking trouble.

Your mother already knows and shes devastated whos this slut, you idiot!

Dad!!!! I meant perfect not pregnant im so sorry. It's this Damn phone, auto-corrected me.

OH... oh god... you just made me piss my pants... son... I broke your laptop...

-_-

LAUNDRY

OMG!!!

NOOO!!!

●●●○○ Verizon 4G   6:23 AM   11%

< Messages   **DAD**   Details

come on down, dinner is ready

> Be there in a min, I'm doing Lauren.

who the fuck is Lauren

if she is your girlfriend, she can have some dinner too.

> Dad! I meant laundry. I'm not a lesbian

that's a shame, men are dicks. now come eat

LAWYER

OMG!!!

NOOO!!!

Dad: Hey, Sexy! The wife is out of town. Kids are still at school. Let yourself in the front door and let's get down! I'm here in bed for you!

Me: Dad, I'm home. And downstairs. You might want to get a hotel and a good lawyer.

Dad: Destroy this text, I was joking around.

MASSAGE

OMG!!!

NOOO!!!

●●●○○ Verizon LTE   9:05 AM   23%

‹ Messages   **Dad**   Details

Can you bring your table over later

My massage table?

Yes. I really need you to rub my sack. It's killing me.

Yeah, you might want mom to do that. Gross.

sack=back. I slept wrong.

Dad, you need a new phone for real

MEAT

OMG!!!

NOOO!!!

•••• Sprint 4G 5:52 PM 10%

< Messages **Dad** Details

There's leftover dinner for you in the fridge

K thanks. How long should I beat the meat?

Not too long or you'll go blind.

Wow. Fail. Heat the meat!

45 seconds on power level 8, you meat beater.

MISTAKE

OMG!!!

NOOO!!!

oooo Verizon LTE 11:16 AM 12%

< Messages **Dad** Details

hey, do you have any condoms I could use? I really need one for tonight.

Dad!?!?! WTF! Do you realize who you just texted?

Ya, I know that I just texted you son. And I also know that you have some. I need one is that ok? I don't want to make the same mistake again.

is the mistake me?

MOTH

NEMO

OMG!!!

NOOO!!!

○○○○ Sprint LTE   6:320 PM   0 8%

⟨ Messages   **Dad**   Details

How's your paper coming along?

> Good… But Finding Nemo came on so I had to take a break.

Do your paper!! It's due TOMORROW!!

> but I HAVE to find Nemo!!!!!

📷 iMessage   Send

NICKNAME

OMG!!!

NOOO!!!

●●●○○ Sprint LTE 9:05 AM 60%

< Messages **Dad** Details

Hey honey, I had fun last night

Dad?

Oh a nickname? Well I guess I'm your daddy ;)

Dad? Wtf? are you cheating on mum?!

Mel ! I meant to send that to Caroline, sorry.

Mum's name is Jessica.

ONIONS

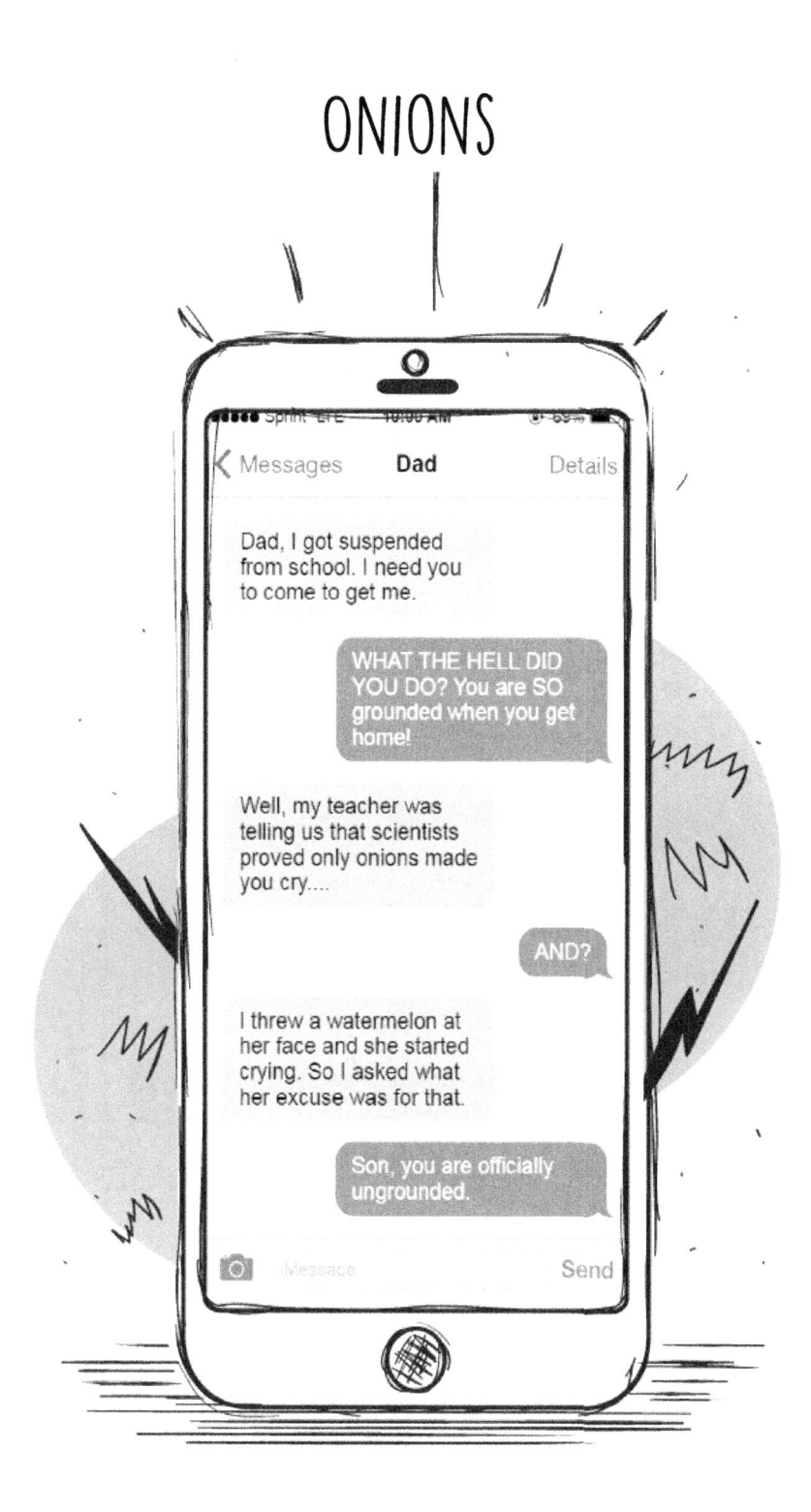

Dad

Dad, I got suspended from school. I need you to come to get me.

> WHAT THE HELL DID YOU DO? You are SO grounded when you get home!

Well, my teacher was telling us that scientists proved only onions made you cry....

> AND?

I threw a watermelon at her face and she started crying. So I asked what her excuse was for that.

> Son, you are officially ungrounded.

OPINION

OMG!!!

NOOO!!!

> Tomorrow's the big day...you'll soon be married. Get some rest, I'll see you in the AM.

> Yeah. Any last-minute advice?

> NEVER EVER tell your wife she's terrible in bed...
>
> She may get a second opinion =/

> Ahhhhh. Laughing. Thanx dad.

PREGNANT

OMG!!!

NOOO!!!

•••○○ Verizon 4G   9:29 AM   34%

‹ Messages   **Dad**   Details

Oh my god! Joe guess what!!!!!

> What?

I,m pregnant!!!!!! :D :D :D

> WHAT! Get home right now young lady! This is your father you are texting! We need to have a little talk!

... Dad, I got married last year and I'm 25...

> Your point?

Message   Send

PREGO

OMG!!!

NOOO!!!

Dad

Mom wants you to get her prego

Well, I can't. I had that problem solved years ago.

OH MY GOD DAD!!!! EW! TMI! I will forever be grossed out. Mom wants you to get her PREGO! The cooking thing.

Oh. Okay sweetie

REALITY

OMG!!!

NOOO!!!

Messages — **Dad** — Details

What do you want for your birthday?

> A girlfriend that's not crazy

You should ask for something more realistic.

Like a dragon.

S3

OMG!!!
NOOO!!!
Verizon 9:57 AM 100%
Messages
Dad
Details
Hey son! Which phone do you like most?
Samsung S3 or iPhone 5?
OMG DAD!!!!!!! I LIKE THE S3 OMG THANKS, DAD!!!
It is not for you. It's for your sister.
Text Message
Send

SCIENCE

OMG!!!

NOOO!!!

> Dad, is Tina on the period?

>> umm how should I know?

> You're a science teacher.

>> Because of that, I am supposed to know when your friend has her period?

> Dang it!!!!!!!!! I meant is Tin on the Aperiodic table

>> oooohhh. Yes. Yes, it is. :)

SHOTGUN AND SHOVEL

OMG!!!

NOOO!!!

> **Dad**
>
> You Asshole! I can't believe you cheated on me!!! You better RUN!!!!!
>
> Oh sorry, dad I meant to send that to Derek...
>
> > Oh that's OK
>
> > On a completely different topic, have you seen my shotgun and my shovel?
>
> Actually I have them both.
>
> > That's my girl

SMILE

OMG!!!

NOOO!!!

●●●●● Sprint 3G   11:29 AM   13%

‹ Messages   **Dad**   Details

Hey, Dan, I can't wait to see your 8====D tonight xoxo

> Ashley, check who you're texting - this is your father. And I know what 8====D means.

What does it mean then?

> it's a smile, of course

That's right Dad!

> ...like the smile on my face when I see you segregated in the house and not out playing with Dan's 8===D

SONS

OMG!!!

NOOO!!!

> son, your mom is terrible in bed, know anywhere to get some hookers?

> WTF

> sorry, I meant to send that to my other son

> HAVE A BROTHER?!

STRIP CLUB

OMG!!!

NOOO!!!

Hey Dad, I have a confession to make.

What son?

I went to a strip club last weekend.

Oh, Did you see anything you weren't supposed too?

Yeah... Mom. o_0

SUCK

> Did you call?

> yeah wanted to tell you your mother sucked my dick up in the vacuum

> What??? Just... What???

> she sucked my dick up and it's gone, wanted to tell you before you saw it was missing.

> Are you on drugs? Are you ok?

> oh, I just read what I wrote and that's not what I meant.

> she sucked my DITKA up. sorry

SWEAR

OMG!!!

NOOO!!!

Dad

I'm at Karen's house

> I don't know *if* I can believe you.
>
> you lie to me all the time.
>
> You know it is not good to lie to your father.

It is the truth

I swallow

SWEAR. Swear. I typed swear.

> COME HOME NOW.

117

TALKING

OMG!!!

NOOO!!!

> Dad, I got suspended

> What happened this time, your grounded

> Well, I was talking in class and the teacher said "Why are you talking while I'm teaching" and I said "Why are you teaching when I'm talking"

> You are un-grounded for learning my smartass talent!

TEA

THE BUTCHER

OMG!!!

NOOO!!!

> don't forget to pick up the turkey breast

> and be sure the butcher has boner

< Um. How can I tell for sure? I mean, should I pull his pants down and check

> be sure, the butcher has it boner lol

> phone won't let me type de boned!

< Wow dad lol 2 very different things! Haha

THE CANNIBAL

OMG!!!

NOOO!!!

•••○○ Verizon 4G   11:31 AM   33%

< Messages   **Dadster**   Details

you there Shawn

> Yea what up daddy-o

I am eating your mother out tonight at 7 so you have to find your own dinner

> Not sure how to respond to that. Uh, have fun?

I'm not eating her out, I'm eating her out

> Oh that clears it up

I mean taking, well this has been a fun chat

THE EXCUSE

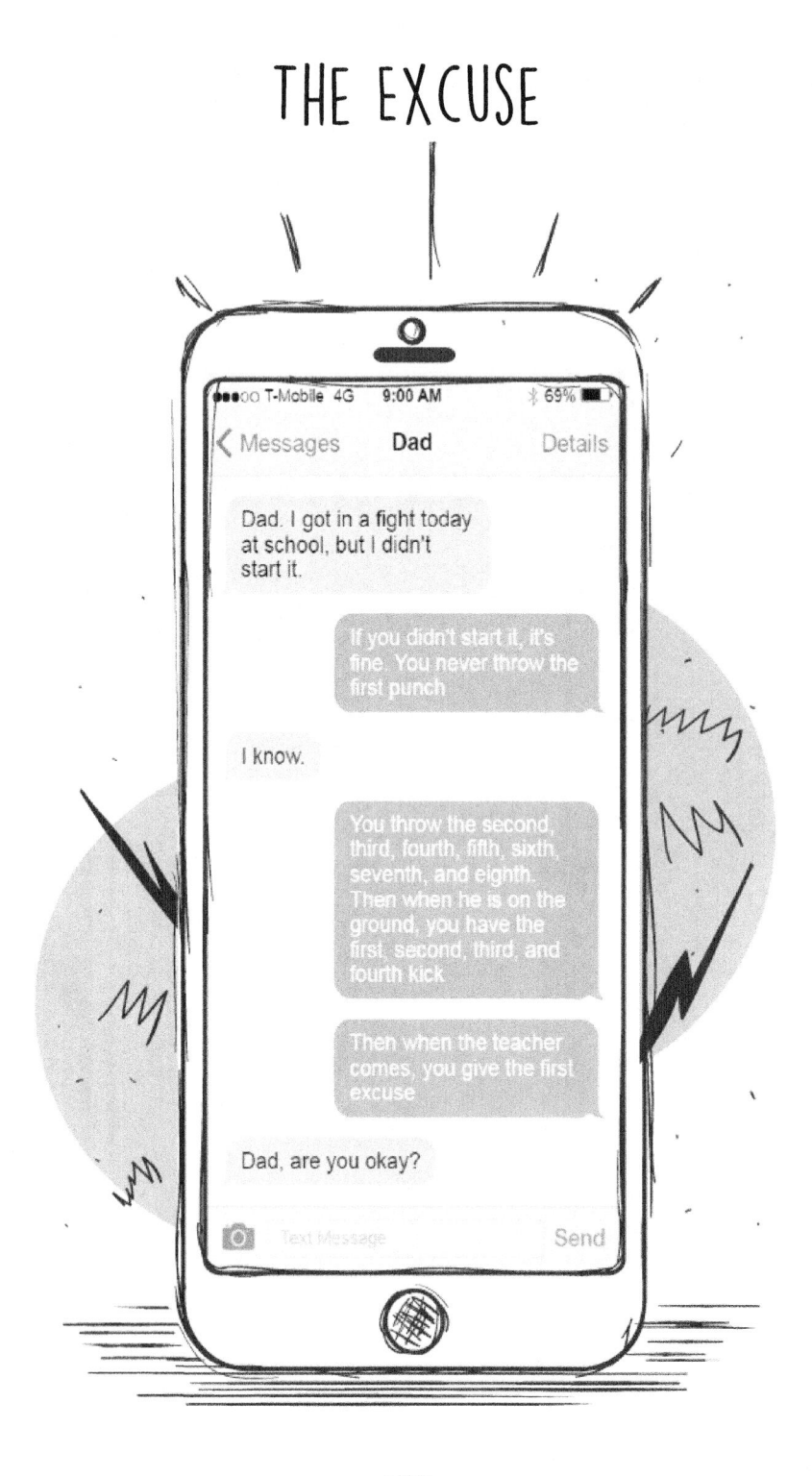

Dad

Dad. I got in a fight today at school, but I didn't start it.

> If you didn't start it, it's fine. You never throw the first punch

I know.

> You throw the second, third, fourth, fifth, sixth, seventh, and eighth. Then when he is on the ground, you have the first, second, third, and fourth kick

> Then when the teacher comes, you give the first excuse

Dad, are you okay?

THE HAND

OMG!!!

NOOO!!!

●●●●● Sprint LTE   4:26 PM   100%

‹ Messages   **Dad**   Details

Hey son. Do you need anything from the store, while I'm here??

Yeah... Can you pick me up some condoms? I have a date tonight...

Son...

Yeah, Dad?

You realize that you can't get your hand pregnant...

THE KEY

OMG!!!

NOOO!!!

Dad

Going out with your mother. See you later.

> Wait how am I supposed to get in the house??

Magic. You put your cock in the hole and turn it. Voila.

> Hahaha, fail dad.

Key you wise ass. I'm sure you are familiar with putting tiny things in holes.

> Ooh. Burn.

THE RULER

Dad I got suspended from school.

WHAT?! Why??

The teacher pointed a ruler at me and said there is an idiot at the end of this ruler.. So I asked which end :)

You are totally my son!

VACUUMING

OMG!!!

NOOO!!!

Dad

Busy Dad?

No, just finished vacuuming

That hooker you left here has some serious sucking powers

DAD! LMAO I think you meant "Hoover"

Anyway, do you want to go grab dinner?

I can't believe that just happened. I thought those auto-corrects were fake.

WEED

WHATS UP

OMG!!!

NOOO!!!

Dad

Hey dad whats up?

Gas prices?

No, I mean what are you doing?

Your mom.

...

WHY ARE YOU GOING THERE

NOOO!!!

OMG!!!

Dad

I'm going to a party

Will you be drinking?

No

Will you be doing drugs?

No

Will you be having sex?

No

Then why the fuck are you going?

*** WIFE AND HUSBAND TEXT FAILS ***

BABY SITTER

OMG!!!

NOOO!!!

Sprint 3G   9:37 AM   8%

‹ Messages   **John**   Details

Did you guys eat dinner yet?

Yep. Just had pasta.

Oh, by the way, I laid the babysitter.

Uh, excuse me? You fucking what?????

Hahaha PAID. I paid her. Sorry to give you a heart attack babe.

hate you! lol

BEARS

OMG!!!

NOOO!!!

Allison

Why is there a bowl of gummy bears on our counter? And they smell like vodka.

Don't touch them. They're masturbating

Don't worry I will not be touching anything that's Masturbating

"Marinating"

I'm making vodka bears!

BROTHER

I'm pregnant!

Omg! Really?!? I'm so happy! I've been wanting to be a dad for a while!

Yeah, I'm very scared how am I going to tell my husband? Peter, please advise me on what to do.

WTF?!? This is Mark, your HUSBAND!! You slept with my brother?!?

OMG!!!

NOOO!!!

CHIHUAHUA

OMG!!!

NOOO!!!

Sprint 4G 9:21 AM 65%

< Messages **Justin** Details

Calm down, crazy. Whatever it is, Justin. I like him. He's sweet. I want to keep him.

YOU CAN'T KEEP A COYOTE. NOBODY DOES THAT.

Stop text yelling at me. You're freaking out for no reason

NO REASON?! THERE'S A COYOTE IN MY HOUSE AND MY LADY IS ACTING LIKE ITS A CHIHUAHUA. YOU HAVE LOST YOUR MIND.

COMPARISON

OMG!!!

NOOO!!!

Lyndsie

I want us to be like Selena and Justin.

> Babe, they broke up

ok fine. Seal and Heidi.

> uh... They split too.

Britney and Justin.

> They split like 10 years ago

Obviously, you're not catching on. It's over.

DINNER

OMG!!!

NOOO!!!

●●●●● T-Mobile 4G　3:49 PM　15%

‹ Messages　**Katy**　Details

I'm making you dinner tonight

Is that so!

Yep! And you're gonna love my chicken flatulence.

Oh god oh god oh god. My chicken florentine.

Not flatulence.

Haha. Um, maybe we should just order a pizza :)

DIVORCED

OMG!!!

NOOO!!!

> Hey, I don't think this is really working. I'm breaking up with you.

> I'm your wife..you can't exactly break up with me. I'm living in your house. You could just walk over to the other side of the room and tell me you want to get divorced.

> Oops, sorry. That was meant for someone else.

> Oh ok :)

> Wait... WHAT!?!?

HAPPY BIRTHDAY

OMG!!!

NOOO!!!

•••○○ Verizon 4G   9:01 AM   @ ● ☒ 55%■

⟨ Messages   **Scott**   Details

Happy Birthday to you!
Happy Birthday to you!
Happy Birthday dead
husband! Happy Birthday
to you!

Thanks. I assume you meant "dear."

Ahhhhh

Yes!!!! I mean that is a crazy autocorrect! Sorry babe.

iMessage   Send

140

HARRY POTTER

OMG!!!

NOOO!!!

●●●○○ AT&T 4G   9:37 AM   11%

< Messages   **Jill**   Details

What movie are you renting tonight?

> Harry Potter

Which one?

> Harry Potter and the deadly halitosis

> HAHAHA Deathly hallows I'm dying

That just happened! LMAO

MONDAY

PRESENT

OMG!!!

NOOO!!!

> Hoah
>
> Hey, did you get Orla her birthday present yet?
>
> > She said she didn't want a present from me
>
> What?
>
> > She said all she wanted from me at her party was my presence
>
> You Idiot! She meant present!

SICKNESS

OMG!!!

NOOO!!!

> Love u

> How's the morning sickness?

> Not too bad today. I can't believe that we're having another baby :)

> I'm leaving you

> What???

> now. I'm leaving work NOW. I am NOT leaving you!

> Now I'm really gonna throw up

THE DRUNK

OMG!!!

NOOO!!!

> Jake u were SO drunk last night at the party.

> No, I wasn't

> O ya, u called a taxi to take u home

> So I don't want to get a ticket for being drunk and driving

> The party was at our house

THE FINGER

OMG!!!

NOOO!!!

Julian

How did Emily break her finger?

> Her finger got stuck in my butthole

WHATTTT?!

> Holyshit. My buckle. Belt buckle.

That is the funniest thing I have heard ALL day!

146

THE OIL

OMG!!!

NOOO!!!

Sheila

I just bought the kids a tramp oil! They're delighted!

Huh?

They're finally playing together! I just hope Jake isn't too rough

OMG, I bought them a trampoline! Autocorrect is gonna get me arrested one day!

THE POET

OMG!!!

NOOO!!!

Miriam

If you are sleeping, send me your dreams.

If you are laughing, send me your smile.

If you are eating, send me a bite.

If you are drinking, send me a sip.

If you are crying, send me your tears.

I love you.

> I'm on the toilet. Please advise.

THE TRUTH

OMG!!!

NOOO!!!

Tyler

whats up babe

> Nothin, I was just thinking about how much I hate your baldspot.

wow. okay, well if we are being honest

I hate your saggy tits and your fat ass.

> What the fuck Ty?? I wrote bosssss and it fucking autocorrected

> You fucking asshole

this is awkward.

*** GRANDPARENTS TEXT FAILS ***

GRANDPARENTS

FOLLICLES

OMG!!!

NOOO!!!

●●●○○ T-Mobile 3G 11:02 AM 81%

< Messages **Granpa** Details

Hey son, I haven't seen you in awhile. Just got this new phone, and texting is fun! how you been? Still, dating that cute girl?

> Haha! Great! And yes

She smells nice? That's how you know she's clean.

> Um.. yes? My gf smells great lol

Your GF? Does that stand for genital follicles?

> Grandpa, you really shouldn't be texting...

153

GOOD NEWS

OMG!!!

NOOO!!!

Messages **Granpa** Details

hi grandpa! I just wanted to know how you are doing? :)

Good. My friends keep dying.

GRANNY

OMG!!!

NOOO!!!

•••• Verizon LTE 11:02 PM 9%

‹ Messages **Grandma** Details

Man, fuck this. I'm tired of your shit. I thought I trusted you, but then you go and do that? Sleep with my girlfriend? FUCK YOU!

Oh, grandma, I'm so sorry. I meant to send that to my friend.

Beat his ass! I'll get the crowbar. I'll fuck up the girl, while you kill your 'friend'.

HELP

OMG!!!

NOOO!!!

Dean

I'm getting murdered!

Oh shit! I'll send for help

Lol, that was autocorrected. I'm getting married!

Oh shit! I'll send for help!

KILL ME

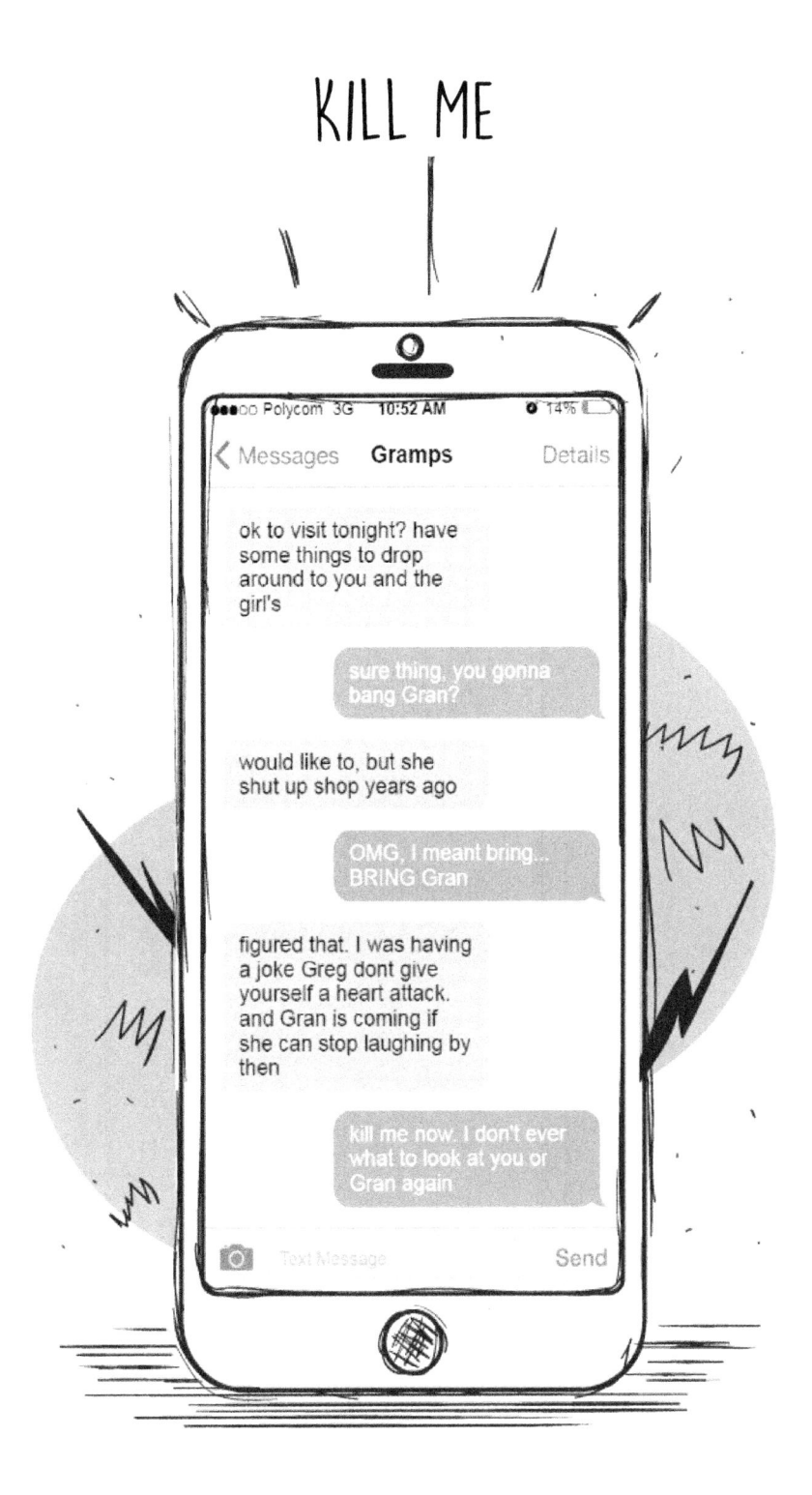

Gramps

ok to visit tonight? have some things to drop around to you and the girl's

> sure thing, you gonna bang Gran?

would like to, but she shut up shop years ago

> OMG, I meant bring... BRING Gran

figured that. I was having a joke Greg dont give yourself a heart attack. and Gran is coming if she can stop laughing by then

> kill me now. I don't ever what to look at you or Gran again

LICK BALLS

OMG!!!

NOOO!!!

●●●○○ Sprint LTE   12:52 AM   9%

‹ Messages   **Granpa**   Details

Yes, I need more medicine but don't go there, they don't have the brand I like.

Sorry honey, that's where I'm stopping. I can't help it you lick balls

I wasn't aware I do that

Like halls

The silly phone is too much for me

PRESIDENT

OMG!!!

NOOO!!!

Grandma I just got elected president!

Oh my goodness! Of the USA?

Haha No grandma, class president

Oh...

Grandma?

Grandma?

TANDEM

OMG!!!

NOOO!!!

Granny Dee

Hi Granny, I'm doing a project for school. Did you ever use a condom?

> Not really dear. They weren't very popular back then. Grandpa used to just pull out

Ewww, Granny! I meant to type tandem! Like the bike!

> Oh no, they were never of much interest to me. I was usully too sore.

160

*** BOYFRIENDS TEXT FAILS ***

BOYFRIENDS

BROKEN BONES

OMG!!!

NOOO!!!

Adam

If you break my heart ill break your Xbox..

Why the Xbox?

Do you want broken bones?...

No..?

Good. I saw you making out with Amanda at the party.. Enjoy your last 15 minutes of MW3...I'll be over soon.

FUCK

BROTHER

OMG!!!

NOOO!!!

●●●○○ T-Mobile 4G   8:11 AM   ❋ 10%

< Messages   **Bestie**   Details

I heard you like my brother, is that true?

> Yes, it is... please don't tell him about it. I hope you aren't mad or anything. I've liked him for a while now.

I'm not mad, he actually knows about it. I think he likes you too.

> WHAT?!?! HOW did he find out?!

You are talking to him right now. I borrowed Sarah's phone because I lost mine yesterday. Pick you up at 8? :)

> Sure <3

BYE BYE

OMG!!!

NOOO!!!

●●●○○ Sprint 3G   6:35 PM   @ ⚡ 53% ▰

‹ Messages   **Chloe**   Details

I just left and we got in a huge fight. She's such a fucking bitch.

I can't wait to see you later though, you can make me forget about her ;)

John, this is Chloe, your girlfriend....or should I say ex girlfriend.

CONDOM

OMG!!!

NOOO!!!

•••○○ Sprint 4G   1:13 PM   43%

< Messages   **Jake**   Details

Heyy babe!! Can't wait to see your 8 D tonight(;

Hi, this is Jake's father. Do you and Jake need some condoms? I took his last one...Oh, and we won't be at home tonight so the house is yours!

Uh...

Wtf?

Oh... I made this awkward didn't I. No worries! I'll just slip one into the drawer.

Message   Send

CONTACTS

DO WE REMAIN FRIENDS

> Look, I really liked u, but now, I just don't have feelings for u anymore. I'm sorry. Do we remain friends?

> R U KIDDING ME ?!? Wow bitch. Just yesterday you tole me u loved me. Guess that didn't mean shit. And ovr Text. W-o-w. W/e.

> OMG DAREN. I didn't mean to send that to u! I meant to send that to my other boyfriend. I love you.

> Ohh, haha Wait for WTF?? U have another boyfriend besides me??

> ...Not anymore. Remember? I'm sending him the breakup msg?

DREAMS

OMG!!!

NOOO!!!

Cris

Hey. You were in my dream last night

Omg you were in mine too

In mine, we lived on a farm and had six kids and a pet unicorn.

Awww <33

And in yours?

...you died in the fire.

DUMPING

OMG!!!

NOOO!!!

●●●○○ T-Mobile LTE   1:13 PM   @ ☼ ✳ 100%

‹ Messages   **Jason**   Details

Be warned: I'm dumping you when I get home tonight.

> Fine with me. I was just thinking we could use some time apart.

WTF JENNA??? I got autocorrected. I meant to write jumping you not dumping you

And now you're telling me x you want to break up?

> Well, this is awkward.

EMO

OMG!!!

NOOO!!!

OMG I am dating that new hot emo dude I think im in love

Umm?

What!?! ohh shit

Its ok babe im in love with you too

Omg I just txt corey and he said he loves me oh we will be together forever... wut do u think jesse? is he perfect for me?

Yes I am

END OF STORY

OMG!!!

NOOO!!!

●●○○ Sprint LTE   2:04 PM   75% ■

< Messages   **Christian**   Details

I love you. <3 <3

> love you more. Always. End of story <3

Oh If Its the end of story then okay, byeeee.

> No! I was kidding! I love you(: <3

No really. End of story. I've been fucking Heather for like 3 weeks LOL.

> Tell your "best friend" Colby that I want my thong back from under his bed. And tell Noah that I'll need my 2 bras back. Fuck you and have a nice . <3

Text Message   Send

HEART ATTACK

OMG!!!

NOOO!!!

Pamela

Can't wait to see you babe. Hurry up and get here!

> Whoo hoo! It's Friday. Screw the gym! I'm getting pregnant tonight!

Uh... Shouldn't we talk about that first?

> HAHAHAHAHA Oh my god.

> I wrote pringles and it autocorrected to pregnant

I almost had a heart attack

INVENTORY

OMG!!!

NOOO!!!

○○○○ Sprint LTE 5:22 AM 34%

< Messages **Betty** Details

Hey Boo! I'm working a little late tonight...:(

...Are you sure you're working late?

Yeah, we're doing inventory.

think you're out with Mark again and still cheating on me.

Nothing's going on! We talked about this in therapy. I can't believe you keep doubting me!

I'm across the bar with my boss Look up.

Text Message Send

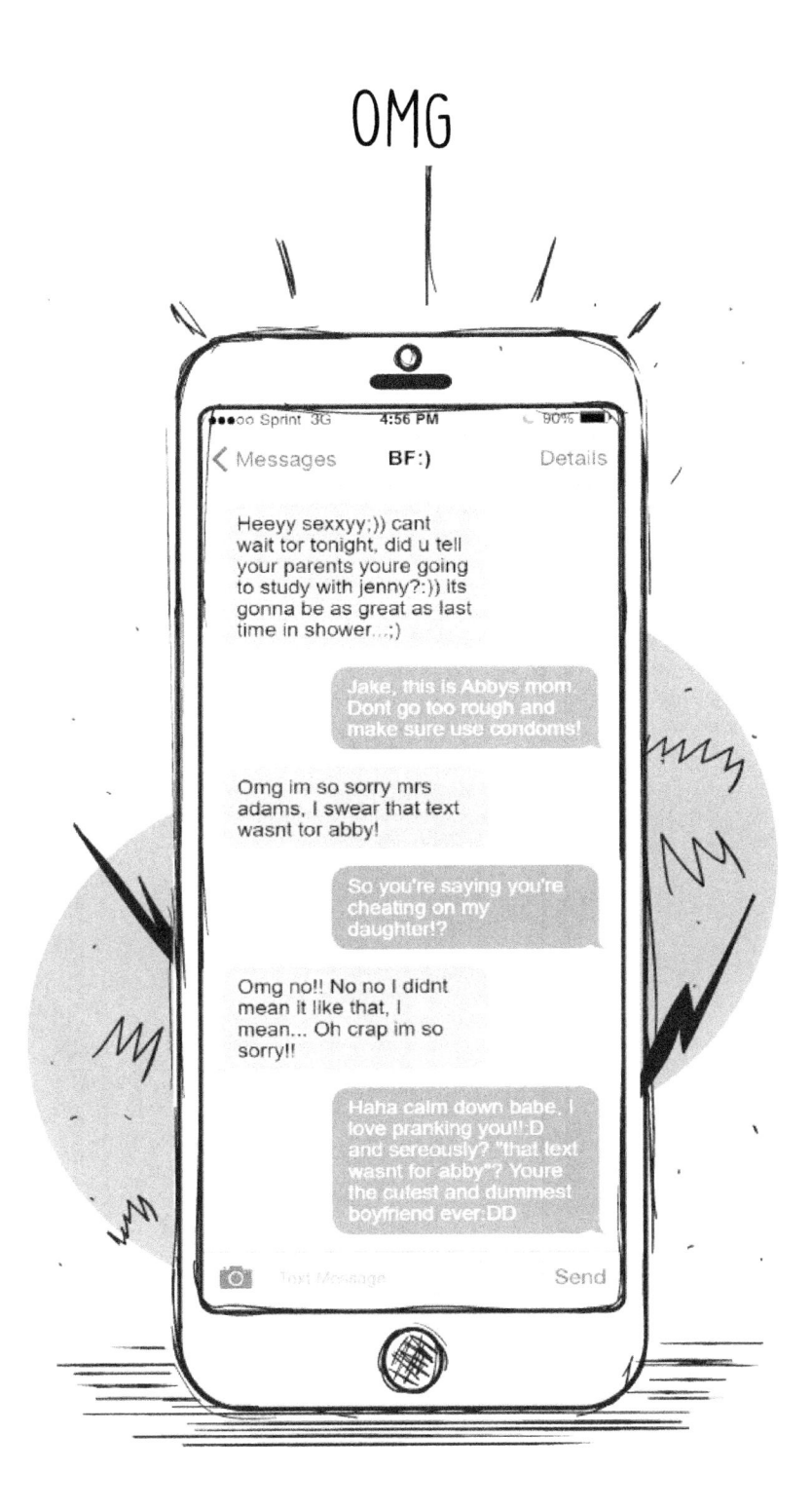

OMG

BF:)

Heeyy sexxyy;)) cant wait tor tonight, did u tell your parents youre going to study with jenny?:)) its gonna be as great as last time in shower...;)

> Jake, this is Abbys mom. Dont go too rough and make sure use condoms!

Omg im so sorry mrs adams, I swear that text wasnt tor abby!

> So you're saying you're cheating on my daughter!?

Omg no!! No no I didnt mean it like that, I mean... Oh crap im so sorry!!

> Haha calm down babe, I love pranking you!!:D and sereously? "that text wasnt for abby"? Youre the cutest and dummest boyfriend ever;DD

PAIN OLYMPICS

OMG!!!

NOOO!!!

> Hello :)
>
> > Oh, hey Mark. What's up?
>
> Oh, this isn't Mark. This is his other girlfriend, Zoey. Apparently, he's been cheating on both of us for a little more than two years.
>
> > Oh, is that so? Well, I just so happen to have seen PainOlympics, if you know what I mean.
>
> ....I have a feeling we're going to be very good friends.
>
> > I'll meet you at his place in ten.

PERMISSION

OMG!!!

NOOO!!!

Hey babe! Wanna come over tonight?

I'll be there in 5!

Don't forget the condoms. ;)

What!? I thought we were just gonna watch movies and play monopoly like always.

This is Kayla's dad. You have my permission to date her.

STARS

OMG!!!

NOOO!!!

> How much do you love me?

> Well, look at the stars and count them. That's how much I love you.

> But It's morning.

> Exactly.

TO SHAVE

OMG!!!

NOOO!!!

My Girl

I'm so glad you texted me baby girl I've been thinking about you all day <3

oh you have?

Yes, I think about you all the time it never stops. All my friends say bros before hoes but I don't care you're not a hoe. you're my number one. This might be too soon, but I love you. Happy six months.

well this is awkward...but i'm leaving you for brad, he shaves his balls

XBOX

OMG!!!

NOOO!!!

•••○○ Sprint LTE 4:34 PM @ 17%

< Messages **BF** Details

Hey baby

What do you want?

Whoa!!! I cheat on my girlfriend for you and you talk to me like that?

You're cheating on me?! Look who you're texting!!!!!!!

... I love you?

I'm taking your Xbox with me.

iMessage Send

ZOMBIES

OMG!!!

NOOO!!!

> **Jane**
>
> Babe... I think I may be pregnant...
>
>> Lol autocorrect. What really happened?
>
> That wasn't a autocorrect.
>
> I'm about 2 months along. I'm sorry 1 didn't tell u sooner.
>
> Ben?
>
>> We need to cause a zombie apocalypse, and get our folks eaten so they'll never know. We'll defeat the zombies and the baby can help repopulate the planet.

*** GIRLFRIENDS TEXT FAILS ***

BALLSACK

OMG!!!

NOOO!!!

●●●○○ Verizon 4G   10:39 AM   ⚡ 20% ▱

‹ Messages   **Matt**   Details

Babe, we need to do something about your ballsack. It reeks down there so bad.

> Wow. That's harsh. I shower 2x a day, I'm not sure what else I can do.

> I feel like shit now. Thanks.

No!!! answer your phone

I wrote basement!!!

You smell fine

Matt?

CLEAN

OMG!!!

NOOO!!!

●●●○○ T-Mobile 3G 1:56 AM 10%

‹ Messages **Blake** Details

Do you remember how when we were together I was really horrible about keeping the house clean??? Well, as it turns out, orgasms really really motivate me to clean.

So you want me to come over and help motivate you?

Lol no, you wouldn't be helpful in the slightest

DRAFT

OMG!!!

NOOO!!!

Sprint 4G 11:56 AM 89%

< Messages **Ryan** Details

So if girls are better than boys, then why did God create man first?

That's obvious. Everyone needs a rough draft before a final copy.

EX

OMG!!!

NOOO!!!

•••○○ Verizon 3G   7:02 PM   92%

< Messages   **Amanda**   Details

Hey, I was just wondering... Uhm what would you do if I broke up with you?

I would go back to my ex :)

Gee thanks. I mean a lot to you. It's over.

Hey, wanna go out? :)

Go with your ex.

You are my ex :)

iMessage   Send

FILM

OMG!!!

NOOO!!!

•••○○ Sprint LTE 22:39 PM 100%

‹ Messages **Ben** Details

Hey, it's over

WTF?!?! Why?! After all, I did for you, this is how you do me u ungrateful jackass!

It's ok, that's why I slept with 3 of your best friends, you prick ass!!

...i was talking bout the movie

oh... how was it?

Fuck you bitch

Text Message Send

189

FIRE

OMG!!!

NOOO!!!

•••○○ Sprint LTE 1:35 AM 75%

< Messages **Stella** Details

Are you up?

...we haven't talked in like 3 weeks

I miss you

And it's cold, I wish we could cuddle.

Oh trust me, if I was there I would warm you right up...by setting you on fire.

Goodnight

GIFT

OMG!!!

NOOO!!!

Paul

Congratulations on getting engaged asshole, I'm never fucking talking to you again!!

So this means you're going to leave me alone?

That's exactly what it means fucker

Best Present. Ever. Thank you!!!!

GIRLFIENDS

OMG!!!

NOOO!!!

•••○○ BellSouth 4G 5:27 PM 87%
< Messages **Jessica** Details

Hey! I miss you :)

who is this?

Um...your girlfriend?
Andy? Are you joking

I'm Andy's girlfriend.

What...? You know what.
Tell Andy we're done.

Will do.

LUBE

OMG!!!

NOOO!!!

oooo Sprint LTE   6:09 AM   25%

‹ Messages   **James**   Details

Hey, dude is it alright if we bang tonight, I'm fed up with my GF and I need a little guy time if you know what I mean ;)

thought you'd never ask. I'll be over tonight, don't worry I got lube

Jesus Christ, I meant hang!!!

oh. yeah, me too

MERRY CHRISTMAS

OMG!!!

NOOO!!!

●●●○○ Sprint 3G   11:42 PM   93%

‹ Messages   **Gabriel**   Details

Merry Christmas Michelle! Love you too :) hope Santa didn't put cock in your stocking

But I love cock!! Lol

Ha Ha Ha Ha Ha oh my god, I meant coal! Holy Jesus

I think that made my morning!!! Lmfao

NOT IN SERVICE

OMG!!!

NOOO!!!

•••• Verizon 4G 9:56 PM 13%

< Messages **Brian** Details

Babe I think I'm Pregnant...

The AT&T Subscriber Yu Are Trying To Reach Is No Longer In Service

You know you spelled "You" WRONG!

The AT&T Subscriber You" Are Trying To Reach Is No Longer In Service

PANTIES

OMG!!!

NOOO!!!

> I have no food here. I'm starving!

> Come over! I've got some tasty stuff in my panties!

> I bet u do HAHAHA

> HAHA, Pantry. Stupid iPhone

> Anyway, come raid my panties

> OMG

POEM

OMG!!!

NOOO!!!

●●●○○ Velzon 4G   3:14 PM   90%

< Messages   **Jhon**   Details

Honey, can you write a poem to me?

Sure ;)

Roses are red, violets are blue, a face like yours belongs to the zoo, but don't worry, I'll be there too! but not in the cage, but laughing at you

That's so cute, wanna see me do a magic trick?

Hahaha, glad you liked it ;) And sure ;)

Poof, you're single :)

Send

SEXY

OMG!!!

NOOO!!!

> **Josh**
>
> Hey, Sexy :)
>
> > Umm, this is Anna I'm pretty sure that was meant for Kellie You know, Kellie, your girlfriend?
>
> Nope, It was mean for you ;)
>
> > Well, that changes things, doesn't it? Aha
>
> Hehe, I won't tell if you don't tell (:
>
> > I don't have to tell. Kellie is reading this over my shoulder

198

TAMPON

OMG!!!

NOOO!!!

●●●○○ AT&T LTE 9:50 AM 14%

‹ Messages   Jenna   Details

For Christ's sake stop leaving the bloody tampon!!!

What?? Where??

Lmfao. The bloody lamp on, in the bathroom. Not The tampon. Laughing so hard. Can not breathe.

Oh my God. I was like WTF? I have my period so I was totally mortified. Lmfao

TWIN

OMG!!!

NOOO!!!

●●●○○ Sprint LTE   2:14 PM   @ ⚡ 25% ▭

⟨ Messages   **Jake**   Details

Omigosh, I feel so bad about cheating on Jake!!

WHAT?!

I know his twin brother tricked me. I feel so awful! D*:

Katie, look who you're texting. It's ok.

Omigosh omigosh I'm soooo sorry!!! D:

It's ok. I still love you forever. My brother, however, is DEAD.

WORK

*** FRIENDS TEXT FAILS ***

ACCIDENT

OMG!!!

NOOO!!!

Gar

Bro I just ran over a guy

> Oh, shit really? Okay just drive away. Cover your license plates and no one will know it was you

LOL Autocorrect! I ran over a dog!

> How the fuck could you do that? You evil bastard! Find the owner right now!

BIRD

OMG!!!

NOOO!!!

I want to buy a pet bird for my mom. Maybe a parrot.

Oh that's cool.

When I was in my 20s I had a COCKATTACK.

Oh didn't we all.

Ahhh hahaha Cockatoo, even!

How many times have you typed cockattack!?

Too many, apparently!!

BLACK AND UPRIGHT

OMG!!!

NOOO!!!

Ellis

Hey, I have a penis I don't use. I know you like them so I thought I'd see if you want it.

Hahahaha ????

It's top of the line. My parents bought it but they never use it. It's black and upright.

Haha Yes I would love your PIANO

BYOP

OMG!!!

NOOO!!!

Hey, I'm having a party tonight. BYOP

Does the P stand for prostitutes?

That should have been a B for Beer.

So the prostitutes will be provided?

CRAIGSLIST

OMG!!!

NOOO!!!

Brand

Dude where are you.

Sorry, bro caught up here with my mom. She asked me to help her sell her vagina on Craigslist

So I'm photographing it and stuff.

You're photographing your mom's vagina? Hahaha TAKE YOUR TIME

Sick man. I meant china.

DENTIST

OMG!!!

NOOO!!!

Dennis

I have had the WORST morning. I had to get root anal

> Really? All the way to the root?

Yeah. The dentist just kept drilling

> Hahaha

What's so funny?

DRIVER

OMG!!!

NOOO!!!

•••• Sprint LTE   10:59 AM   100%

< Messages   **Blake**   Details

Hey, man, can I borrow ur wife's cunt for a couple of hours

Are you fucking serious?

Damn, I've driven it many times bro

I won't be that long

Do u know what u said?

iMessage   Send

FORESKIN

OMG!!!

NOOO!!!

> Hey, I have a massive cut on my foreskin, do you want me to cover it before meeting your parents?

>> Hahaha, How did you get that?

> I hit the head of a wall

>> OMG, You hit the whole head?

> Hahaha I meant say Forehead

>> I'm not sure if I'm disappointed or relieved

HAIR

JITTERS

OMG!!!

NOOO!!!

> Stephanie
>
> I think I've had too much caffeine today. I have the shitters I can't stop
>
> > Shitters? You can't stop shitting??
>
> HAHAHAHA omg I'm laughing so hard right now omg
>
> I meant JITTERS
>
> Stupid autocorrect
>
> > HahahhahahhaHaha holy eff

JUST A WORK

OMG!!!

NOOO!!!

> Harry
>
> Hey, what's up?
>
> > Just a work
>
> I really don't think you should be texting at work
>
> > Why not? You're at work too
>
> Yeah but I'm not a taxi driver

LOBSTER

OMG!!!

NOOO!!!

> So how was the date, last night bro
>
> Did you score

>> not quite. the first date we went to dinner and then walked her home
>>
>> then I killed her in the woods outside her house and left

> Killing her seems a bit harsh. Did she order the lobster and filet mignon at dinner or something?

>> *********Kissed wtf

MEASURE

OMG!!!

NOOO!!!

•••○○ Verizon LTE 10:59 AM 28%

⟨ Messages **Jake** Details

I heard you're going out with my ex. How does the used pussy feal?

> What can I say? After the first two inches, like a new one...

Fuck you...

SISTER

OMG!!!

NOOO!!!

Eric

You should have seen the girl I picked up last night!

Was she hot?

YES!

Hey, I left my wallet in your kitchen will you bring it to me?

Yeah sure, I'll go to your house now

There's no need, just bring it into your sister's room

TESTICLES

OMG!!!

NOOO!!!

oooo Sprint 9:48 AM 83%

< Messages **Sara** Details

Is John still out of work?

Yes, unfortunately. Money is tight.

My youngest son's upset because we sold his testicles at a tag sale.

Well, I'd be pretty that mad at too. Lol.

Gah! Tricycles! LOL. Wow. That was a bad mix up.

Oh, I'll say!

Text Message Send

THE PARTY

OMG!!!

NOOO!!!

•••• Sprint 8:35 AM 66%

< Messages **Jason** Details

Did you figure out where the party is gonna be?

Yea we're just gonna do it at Brandon's place because he has the biggest dick.

Oh my

Yea I saw it last night. It's huge

Hope his "dick" can handle the load

huh?

FUCK DECK!

THE PIC

OMG!!!

NOOO!!!

Travis

Hey

I just emailed you a pic of my penis, did you get it?

> WTF man

Not my penis, my penis

My new penis

Ducking phone, my black penis

> Don't send me that shit

BLACK PUMAS bro

LoL sorry

TITS

OMG!!!

NOOO!!!

> Hey
>
> Hey
>
> Ugh, dude, my mom's tits just popped and I can't do anything tonight...
>
> Lol, wtf!!? Ur moms tits popped?
>
> ***TIRES!!! DYAC!? Ugh I hate this phone

Printed in Great Britain
by Amazon